Pet Care

A RABBIT FOR YOU

Caring for Your Rabbit

Written by Susan Blackaby

Illustrated by Charlene DeLage

Content Advisers: Jennifer Zablotny, D.V.M.

Kerrie Burns, D.V.M.

Reading Adviser: Susan Kesselring, M.A., Literacy Educator

Rosemount-Apple Valley-Eagan (Minnesota) School District

PICTURE WINDOW BOOKS

Minneapolis, Minnesota

Editor: Nadia Higgins
Designer: Nathan Gassman
Page production: Picture Window Books
The illustrations in this book were painted with watercolor.

Picture Window Books
5115 Excelsior Boulevard
Suite 232
Minneapolis, MN 55416
1-877-845-8392
www.picturewindowbooks.com

Printed in the United States of America.
1 2 3 4 5 6 08 07 06 05 04 03

Library of Congress Cataloging-in-Publication Data
Blackaby, Susan.
A rabbit for you : caring for your rabbit / written by Susan Blackaby ; illustrated by Charlene DeLage.
p. cm. — (Pet care)
Contents: All kinds of rabbits—What do rabbits eat?—Where do rabbits live?—Making friends with rabbits—Playing with rabbits—Make a rabbit salad—Fun facts—Rabbit guide.
ISBN 1-4048-0118-9 (lib. bdg.)
1. Rabbits—Juvenile literature. [1. Rabbits as pets.] I. DeLage, Charlene, 1944- ill. II. Title.
SF453.2 .B58 2003
636.9'322—dc21
2002155007

TABLE OF CONTENTS

All Kinds of Rabbits

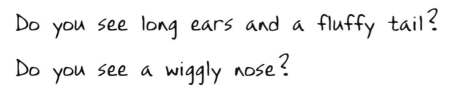

Think of a furry rabbit.

Do you see long ears and a fluffy tail?

Do you see a wiggly nose?

Which kind of rabbit hops into your head?

There are more than 40 different kinds of rabbits!

Rabbits can have ears that are droopy or stumpy.

Rabbits can have noses that are flat or skinny.

Some rabbits have long, fluffy fur.

Some rabbits have short, fuzzy fur.

Rabbit fur can be white, gray, black, or brown.

It can be apricot orange or blue like the night sky.

A rabbit can have spots like a dalmatian.

It can have bands like a raccoon.

It can be white with a dark saddle.

What Do Rabbits Eat?

A rabbit needs to eat a lot of hay.

It needs rabbit pellets and plenty of fruits and vegetables.

A hay rack is a handy place for hay.

A rabbit needs lots of water.

Keep the water bottle full all the time.

Chop Up These Rabbit Snacks
- apples
- broccoli
- carrots
- celery
- parsley
- spinach
- tomatoes
- turnips

Where Do Rabbits Live?

Pet rabbits need an indoor hutch.

The bigger the bunny, the bigger the hutch should be.

HAY

The bottom of a hutch is wire.

The wire can hurt a rabbit's feet.

Put a square of heavy cardboard on the hutch

floor to give your rabbit a comfy place to sit.

Cover the bottom of the hutch with wood shavings or straw.

Rabbits like to dig tunnels. Rabbits like to make nests.

Clean the hutch each week.

Sweep it out and scrub the wire floor with soapy water.

Add new wood shavings or straw.

Making Friends with Rabbits

Your new rabbit might be scared of you.

Talk softly to your rabbit for the first few days.

Then let it eat out of your hand.

Some rabbits like to snuggle, and some don't.

Put a squirmy rabbit down right away.

Its toenails can scratch you as it tries to get away.

How to Pick Up a Rabbit

Put one hand on the back of your rabbit's neck. Use your other hand and arm to lift its bottom. Hold it close to your chest.

Playing with Rabbits

Let your rabbit out of the hutch to exercise regularly.

It might like to follow you around the house.

Your rabbit can also play outside in a pen.

Rabbits like to chew on things they should not eat. Be sure that your rabbit's exercise area is safe. Don't let your rabbit get out of sight.

Let your rabbit get to know your other pets.

Put your rabbit back in the hutch if it seems scared.

Take good care of your furry, friendly rabbit.

It will be a happy, hoppy pet.

Make a Rabbit Salad

This delicious salad looks like rabbits huddling on your plate.

You will need:

one clean leaf of lettuce per serving

one canned pear half per serving

cottage cheese

slivered almonds

raisins

small red cinnamon candy

For each serving:

1. Place one canned pear half, flat side down, on a leaf of lettuce.
2. Put a scoop of cottage cheese next to the wide end of the pear half.
   This will be the rabbit's tail.
3. On the skinny end of the pear half, make the rabbit's face. Use two slivered
   almonds for ears, two raisins for eyes, and one small cinnamon candy for a nose.

Fun Facts

- Baby rabbits are called kittens or kits.
- Rabbits thump the ground if they think danger is near.
  The noise tells other rabbits to look out!
- Rabbits listen for strange sounds. They stand on
  two legs to see what's up.
- You can walk a rabbit on a leash.
- Rabbits can be trained to use a litter box.

Words to Know

hay—dried field grasses

hutch—a cage for a rabbit

pellets—small, dry pieces of food made especially for pets

pen—a small area with a fence around it to keep animals from running away

straw—the dried stems of certain grains. Straw is like hay, only thicker.

Rabbit Guide

There are a lot of kinds of rabbits. This chart tells you about a few of them.

What is its name?	What does it look like?
Angora	An Angora rabbit has long, thick fur.
Dutch	A Dutch rabbit has a white nose and white fur on the back of its neck.
English Lop	An English Lop's ears are so long that it sometimes steps on them.
Flemish Giant	A Flemish Giant is the biggest kind of rabbit— often bigger than a cat.
Holland Lop	A Holland Lop has soft ears that hang down.
Netherland Dwarf	A Netherland Dwarf is the smallest kind of rabbit. It weighs about two pounds (less than one kilogram).
Rex	A Rex rabbit has the softest fur.

23

To Learn More

At the Library

Frost, Helen. *Rabbits*. Mankato, Minn.: Pebble Books, 2001.

Rylant, Cynthia. *Henry and Mudge and Annie's Perfect Pet*. New York: Simon & Schuster Books for Young Readers, 2000.

Tidd, Louise Vitellaro. *The Best Pet Yet*. Brookfield, Conn.: Millbrook, 1998.

Viner, Bradley. *Rabbit*. Hauppauge, N.Y.: Barron's, 1999.

On the Web

ASPCA Kids' Site
http://www.animaland.org
For stories, games, and information about pets

House Rabbit Society
http://www.rabbit.org
For information on choosing and caring for a pet rabbit

Want to learn more about rabbits?
Visit FACT HOUND at *http://www.facthound.com*.

Index